FLASHCARD BOOKS

4 BOOKS IN 1

ANIMALS - HOUSEHOLD ITEMS - CLOTHING - NUMBERS, SHAPE AND COLORS

ENGLISH to JAPANESE

FLASHCARD BOOK

BLACK & WHITE EDITION

HOW TO USE:

• READ THE ENGLISH WORD ON THE FIRST PAGE.

• IF YOU KNOW THE TRANSLATION SAY IT OUT LOUD.

• TURN THE PAGE AND SEE IF YOU GOT IT RIGHT.

• IF YOU GUESSED CORRECTLY, WELL DONE!
IF NOT, TRY READING THE WORD USING THE PHONETIC PRONUNCIATION GUIDE.

• NOW TRY THE NEXT PAGE.
THE MORE YOU PRACTICE THE BETTER YOU WILL GET!

FLASHCARD BOOKS

ANIMALS

ENGLISH to JAPANESE

FLASHCARD BOOK

BLACK & WHITE EDITION

Bat

こうもり

Koumori

Bear

くま

Kuma

Bee

はち

Hachi

Bull

おうし

Oushi

Butterfly

ちょう

Chou

Cat

猫

Neko

Cheetah

ちーたー

Chi-ta

Chicken

にわとり

Niwatori

Cow

うし

Ushi

Crab

かに

Kani

Crocodile

わに

Wani

Dog

犬

Inu

Dolphin

いるか

Iruka

Duck

かも

Kamo

Elephant

ぞう

Zou

Fish

さかな

Sakana

Flamingo

ふらみんご

Furamingo

Fox

きつね

Kitsune

Frog

かえる

Kaeru

Giraffe

きりん

Kirin

Goat

やぎ

Yagi

Goose

がちょう

Gachou

Gorilla

ごりら

Gorira

Hamster

はむすたー

Hamusuta

Hippo

かば

Kaba

Horse

うま

Uma

Iguana

いぐあな

Iguana

Jellyfish

くらげ

Kurage

Kangaroo

かんがるー

Kangaruu

Koala

こあら

Koara

Lady bird

てんとうむし

Tentoumushi

Lion

らいおん

Raion

Manatee

まなてぃー

Manatii

Monkey

さる

Saru

Mouse

ねずみ

Nezumi

Ostrich

だちょう

Dachou

Owl

ふくろう

Fukurou

Panda

ぱんだ

Panda

Parakeet

いんこ

Inko

Parrot

おうむ
Oumu

Penguin

ぺんぎん

Pengin

Pig

ぶた

Buta

Pigeon

はと

Hato

Rabbit

うさぎ

Usagi

Rhino

さい

Sai

Rooster

おんどり

Ondori

Scorpion

さそり

Sasori

Seagull

かもめ

Kamome

Seal

あざらし

Azarashi

Shark

さめ

Same

Sheep

ひつじ

Hitsuji

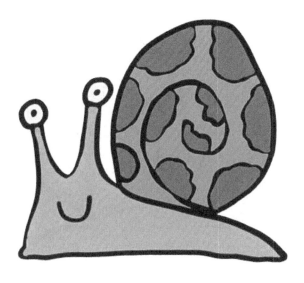

Snail

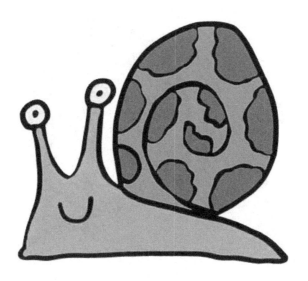

かたつむり

Katatsumuri

Snake

へび

Hebi

Squirrel

りす

Risu

Deer

しか

Shika

Stork

こうのとり

Kounotori

Tiger

とら

Tora

Toad

ひきがえる

Hikigaeru

Tortoise

かめ

Kame

Turkey

しちめんちょう

Shichimenchou

Turtle

うみがめ

Umigame

Wolf

おおかみ

Ookami

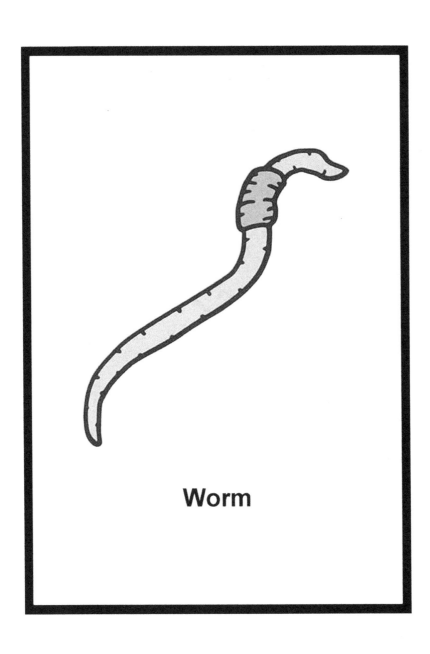

Worm

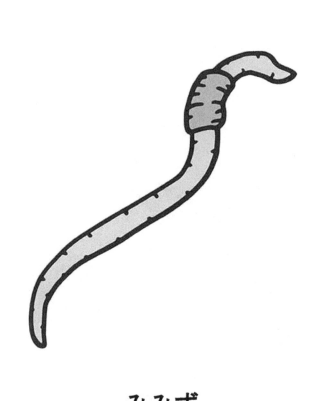

みみず

Mimizu

FLASHCARD BOOKS

CLOTHING

ENGLISH to JAPANESE

FLASHCARD BOOK

BLACK & WHITE EDITION

Baby Bodysuit

ろんぱーす

Ronpa-su

Backpack

りゅっくさっく

Ryukkusakku

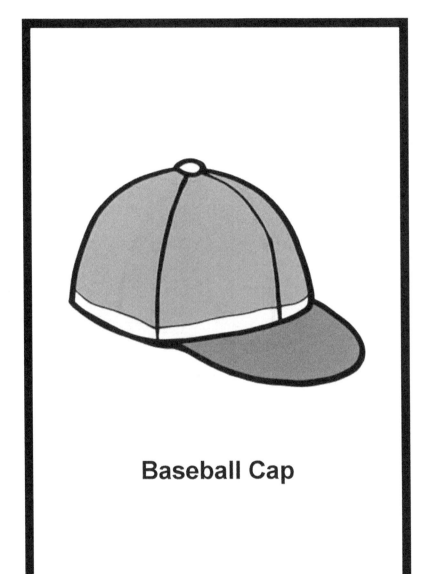

Baseball Cap

やきゅうぼう

Yakyuubou

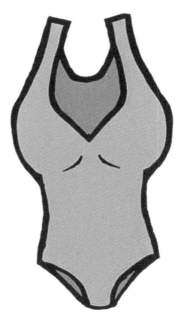

Bathing suit

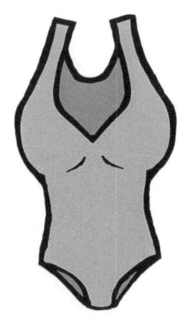

みずぎ

Mizugi

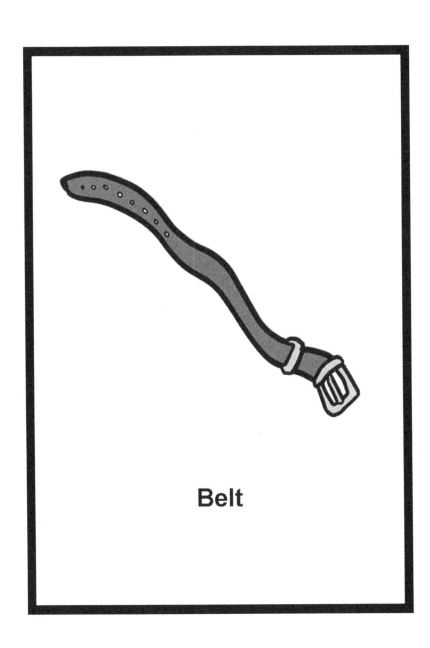

Belt

べると

Beruto

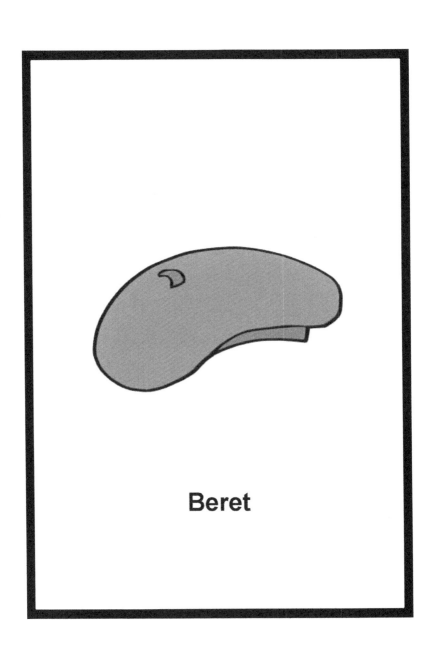

Beret

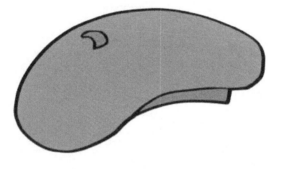

べれーぼう

Bere-bou

Bib

よだれかけ

Yodarekake

Boots

ぶーつ

Bu-tsu

Bowtie

ちょうねくたい

Chounekutai

Boxer shorts

ぼくさーぱんつ

Bokusa-pantsu

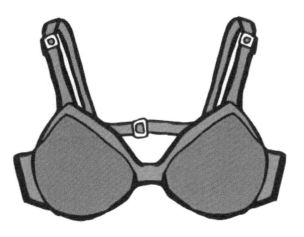

Bra

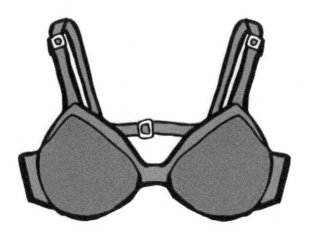

ぶらじゃー

Buraja-

Buttons

ぼたん

Botan

Cardigan

かーでぃがん

Ka-digan

Coat

こーと

Ko-to

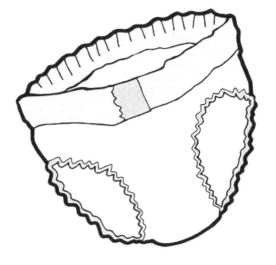

Diaper

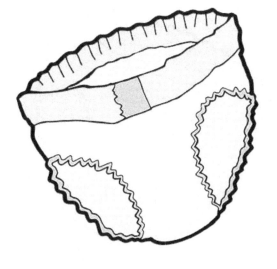

おむつ

Omutsu

Dress

どれす

Doresu

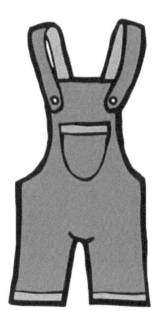

Dungarees

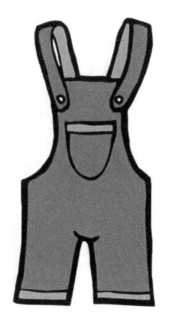

おーばーおーる

O-ba-o-ru

Earrings

いやりんぐ

Iyaringu

Glasses

めがね

Megane

Gloves

てぶくろ

Tebukuro

Handbag

はんどばっぐ

Handobaggu

Hoodie

ぱーかー

Pa-ka-

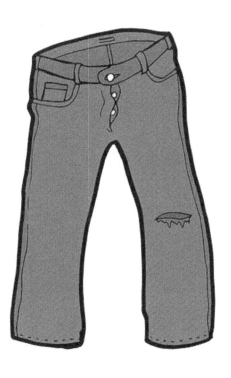

Jeans

じーんず

Ji-nzu

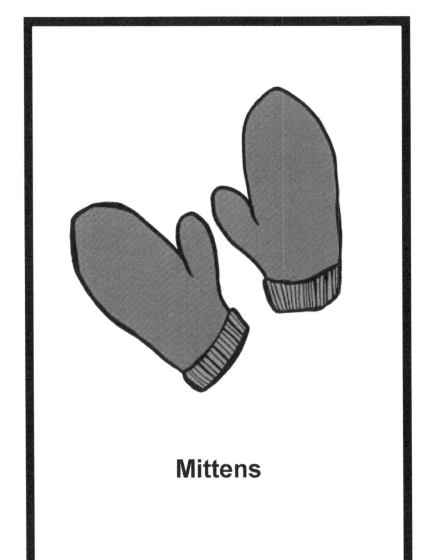

Mittens

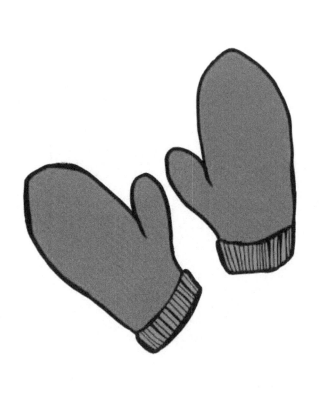

みとん

Miton

Necklace

ねっくれす

Nekkuresu

Pajamas

ぱじゃま

Pajama

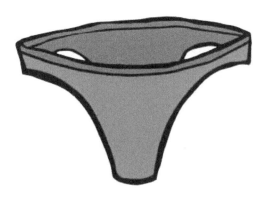

Panties

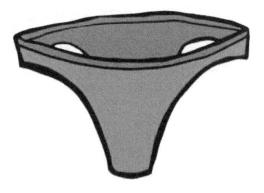

ぱんてぃー

Pantsu

Party Hat

ぱーてぃーはっと

Pa-ti-hatto

Rain Coat

れいんこーと

Reinko-to

Ring

ゆびわ

Yubiwa

Robe

ろーぶ

Ro-bu

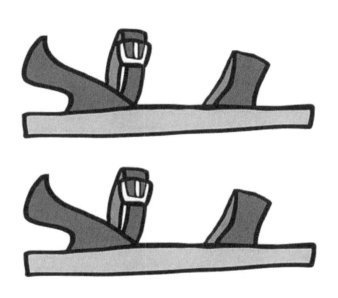

Sandals

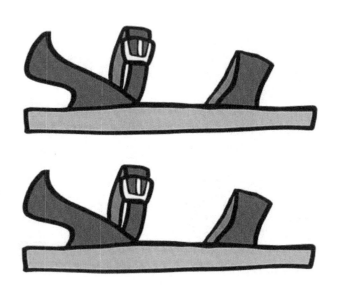

さんだる

Sandaru

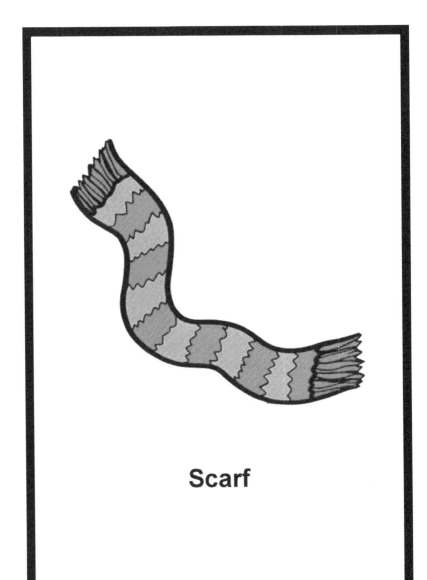

Scarf

すかーふ

Suka-fu

Shirt

しゃつ

Shatsu

Shorts

しょーとぱんつ

Sho-topantsu

Skirt

すかーと

Suka-to

Slippers

すりっぱ
Surippa

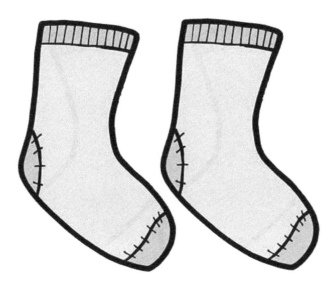

Socks

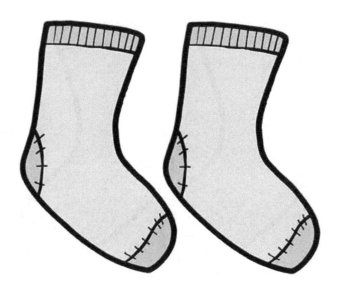

くつした

Kutsushita

Suit

すーつ

Su-tsu

Sunglasses

さんぐらす

Sangurasu

Sweater

せーたー

Se-ta-

Swimming Trunks

かいすいぱんつ

Kaisuipantsu

Tee-shirt

てぃーしゃつ

Tei-shatsu

Tie

ねくたい

Nekutai

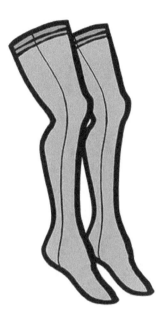

Tights

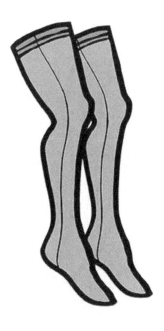

ぱんてぃーすとっきんぐ

Panti-stokkingu

Top hat

しるくはっと

Shirukuhatto

Sneakers

すにーかー

Suni-ka-

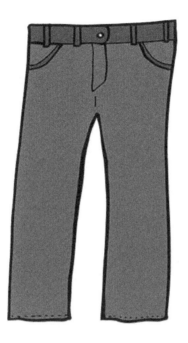

Trousers

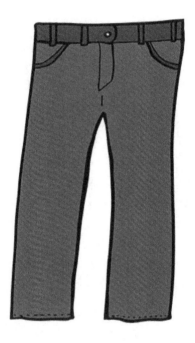

ずぼん

Zubon

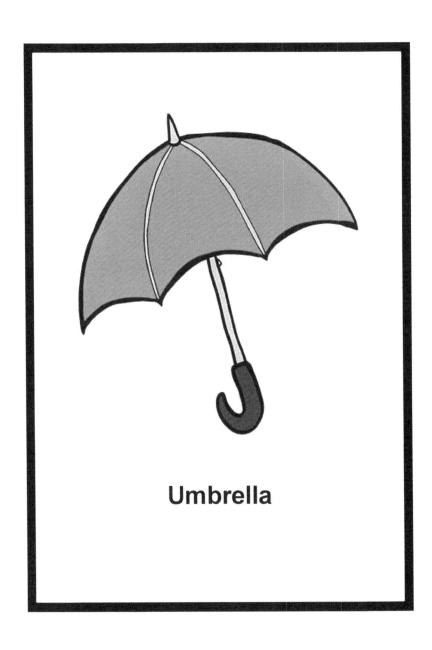

Umbrella

かさ

Kasa

Underpants

ぱんつ

Pantsu

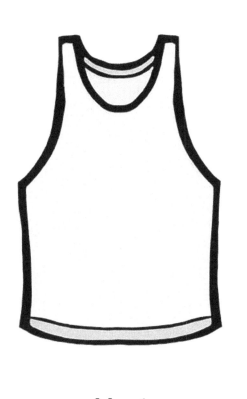

Vest

たんくとっぷ

Tankutoppu

Waistcoat

べすと

Besto

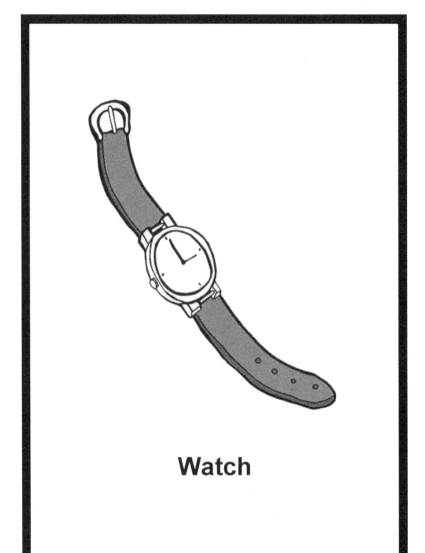

Watch

とけい

Tokei

Wellies

ながぐつ

Nagagutsu

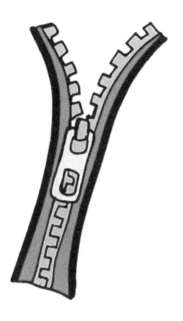

Zip

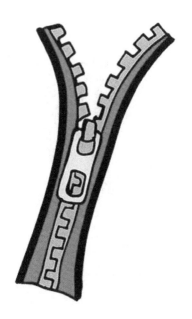

ちゃっく

Chakku

FLASHCARD BOOKS

HOUSEHOLD ITEMS

ENGLISH to JAPANESE

FLASHCARD BOOK

BLACK & WHITE EDITION

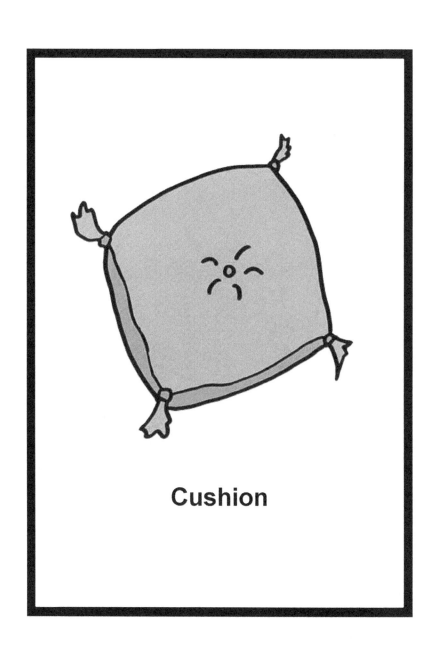

Cushion

クッション

Kusshon

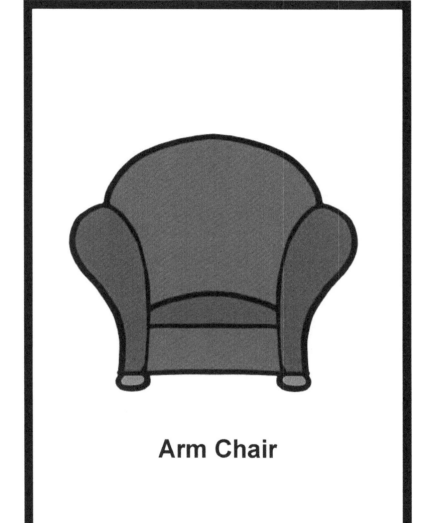

Arm Chair

椅子

Isu

Sofa

ソファ

Sofa

Fireplace

暖炉

Danro

Magazine

雑誌

Zasshi

PC

パソコン

Pasokon

Television

テレビ

Terebi

Remote Control

リモコン

Rimokon

Speakers

スピーカー

Supiikaa

Laptop

ノートパソコン

Nouto pasokon

Fish Tank

水槽

Suisou

Light Bulb

電球

Denkyuu

Rug

カーペット

Kaapetto

Clock

時計

Tokei

Keys

鍵

Kagi

Iron

アイロン

Airon

Plant

植物

Shokubutsu

Table

テーブル

Teeburu

Shelf

棚

Tana

Photo Frame

写真たて

Shashin tate

Light Switch

電気スイッチ

Denki suicchi

Balloon

風船

Fuusen

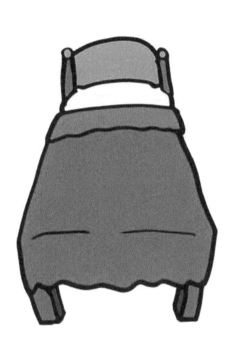

Bed

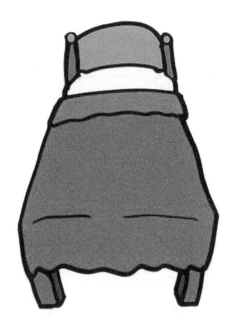

ベッド

Beddo

Double Bed

ダブルベッド

Daburu beddo

Bunk Bed

二段んベッド

Ni dan beddo

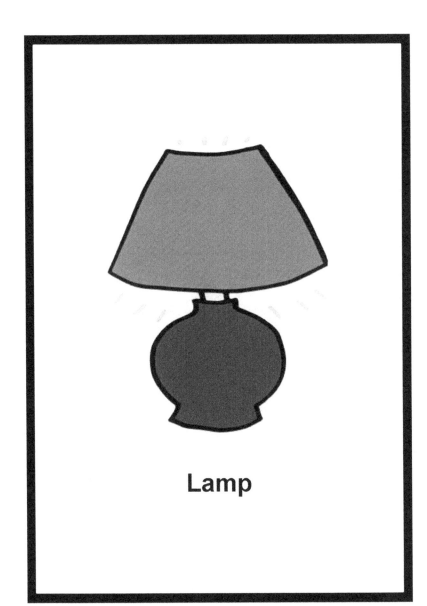

Lamp

ランプ

Ranpu

Pillow

まくら

Makura

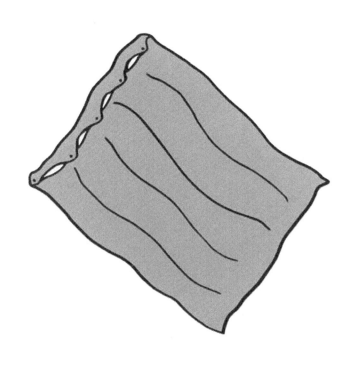

Duvet

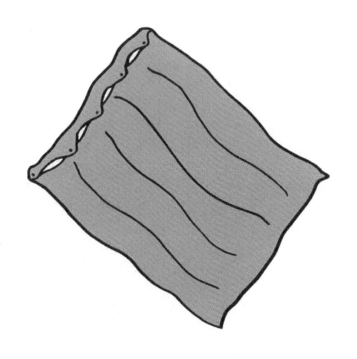

布団のカバー

Futon no kabaa

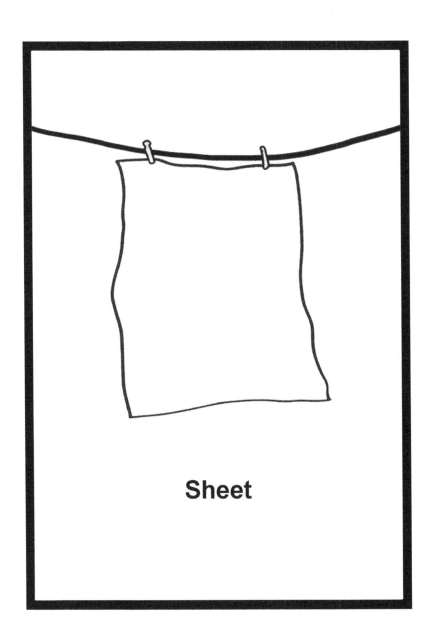

Sheet

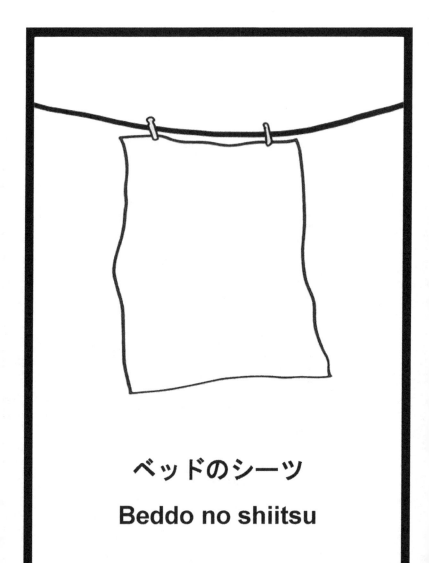

ベッドのシーツ

Beddo no shiitsu

Alarm Clock

目覚まし時計

Mezamashi dokei

Crib

寝床

Nedoko

Wardrobe

洋服ダンス

Youfuku dansu

Drawers

引き出し

Hikidashi

Mobile/Cell Phone

携帯電話

Keitai denwa

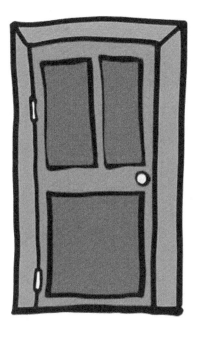

Door

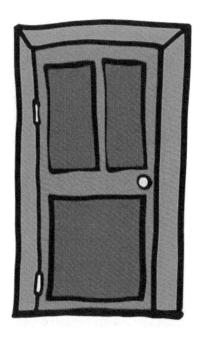

ドア

Doa

Window

窓

Mado

Roof

やね

Ya ne

Door Bell

ドアベル

Doa beru

Newspaper

新聞

Shin bun

Oven

オーブン

Obun

Microwave

電子レンジ

Denshi renji

Toaster

オーブントースター

Obun tosutaa

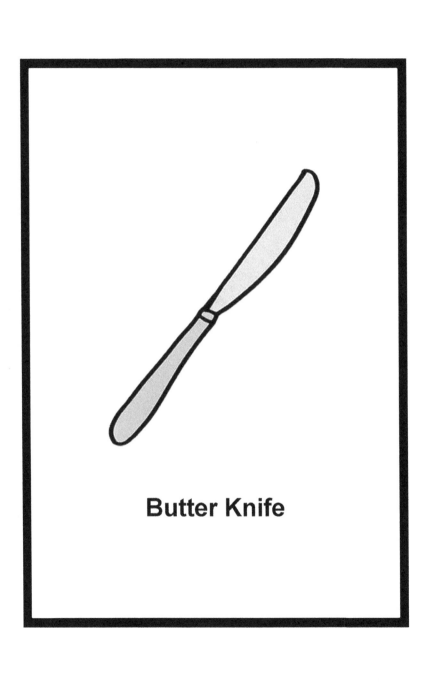

Butter Knife

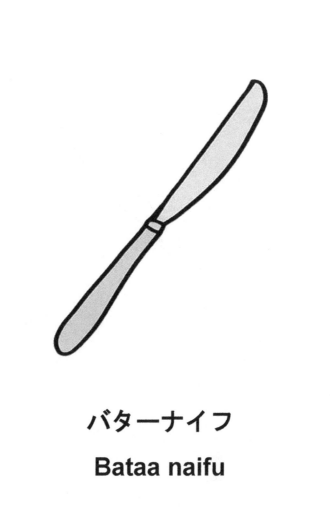

バターナイフ

Bataa naifu

Fork

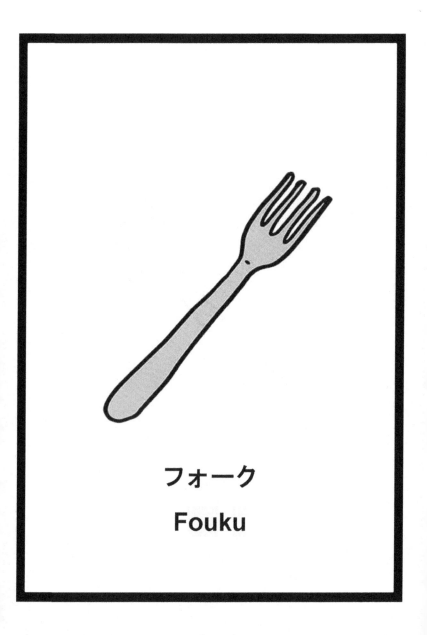

フォーク

Fouku

Spoon

スプーン

Supuun

Kitchen Sink

洗い場

Araiba

Cupboard

戸棚

Todana

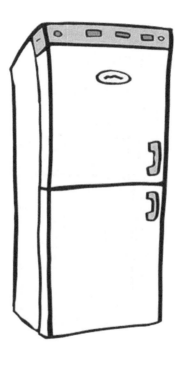

Fridge

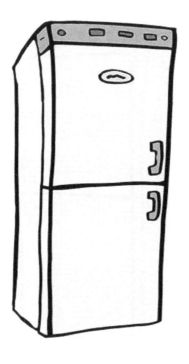

冷蔵庫

Reizouko

Kettle

ケットル

Kettoru

Pans

鍋

Nabe

Frying Pan

フライパン

Furaipan

Knife

包丁

Houchou

Dishwasher

食器洗い機

Shokkiaraiki

Washing up Liquid

洗剤

Senzai

Washing Machine

洗濯機

Sentakuki

Oil

油

Abura

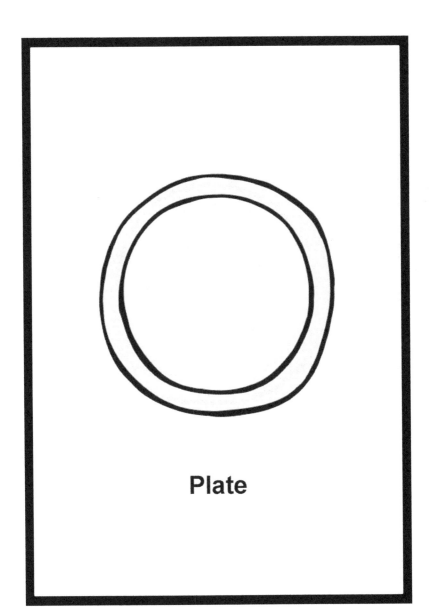

Plate

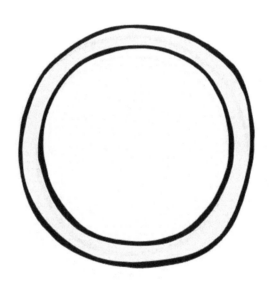

Ⅲ

Sara

Cup

コップ

Koppu

Broom

ほうき

Houki

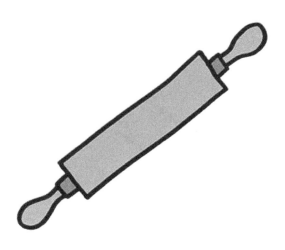

Rolling Pin

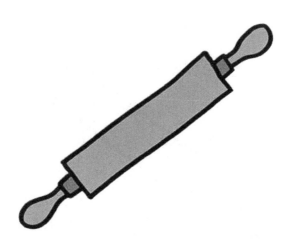

麺棒

Menbou

Toothbrush

歯ブラシ

Haburashi

Toothpaste

歯磨き粉

Hamigakiko

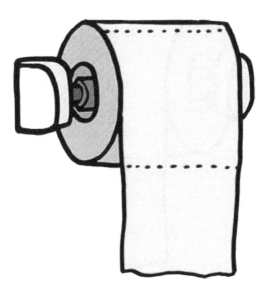

Toilet Paper

トイレットペーパー

Toiretto-peepaa

Shower

シャワー

Shawaa

Soap

石けん

Sekken

Tap

蛇口

Jaguchi

Toilet

トイレ

Toire

Sink

シンク

Shinku

Bath

お風呂

Furo

Shampoo

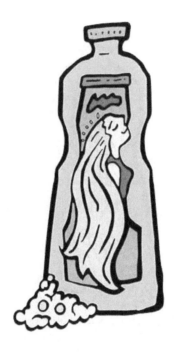

シャンプー

Shanpuu

Sponge

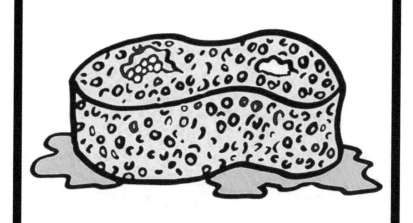

スポンジ

Suponji

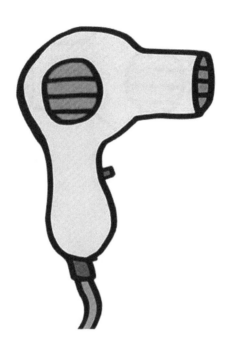

Hairdryer

ドライヤー

Doraiyaa

Pencil Sharpener

えんぴつ削り

Enpitsu-kezuri

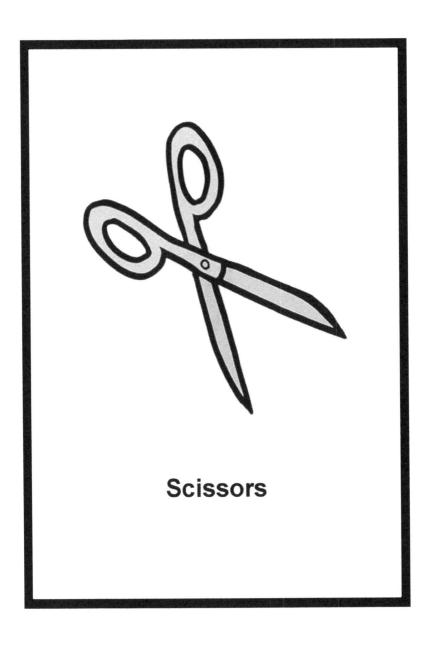

Scissors

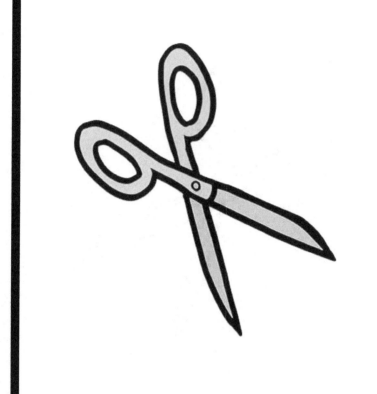

はさみ

Hasami

Book Case

本棚

Hondana

Chair

椅子

Isu

Ball

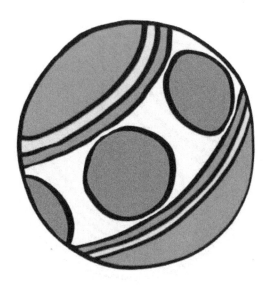

ボール

Bouru

Doll

人形

Ningyou

Teddy Bear

クマのぬいぐるみ

Kuma no Nuigurumi

Castle

お城

Oshiro

Sandwich

サンドイッチ

Sandoicchi

Breakfast Cereal

コーンフレーク

Koun fureeku

Milk

牛乳

Gyuunyuu

Apple

りんご

Ringo

Hammer

金槌

Kanaduchi

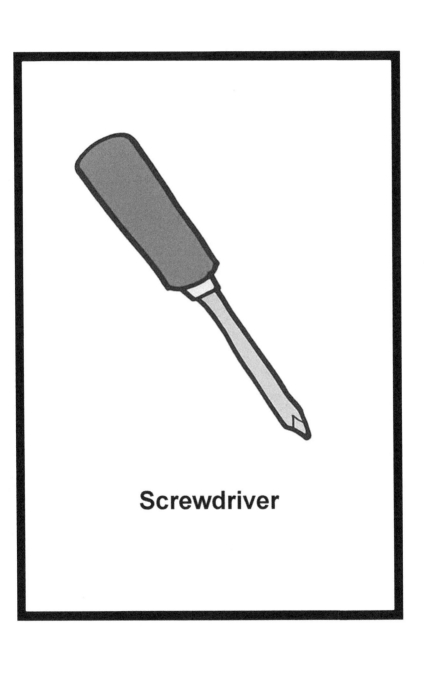

Screwdriver

ドライバ

Doraiba

Screw

ネジ

Neji

Nails

釘

Kugi

Wrench/Spanner

スパナ

Supana

Shovel

スコップ

Sukoppu

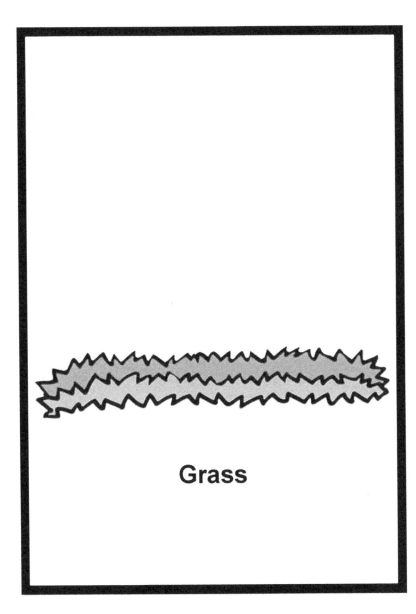

Grass

草

Kusa

Tree

木

Ki

Green House

温室

Onshitsu

Lawn Mower

草きり機

Kusa kiri ki

Hose

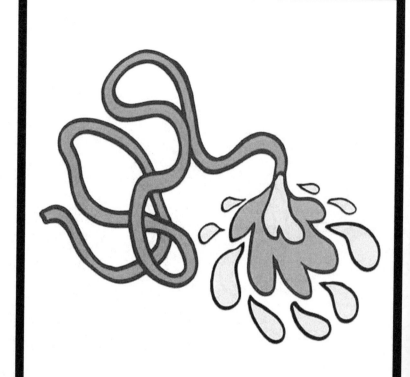

ホース

Housu

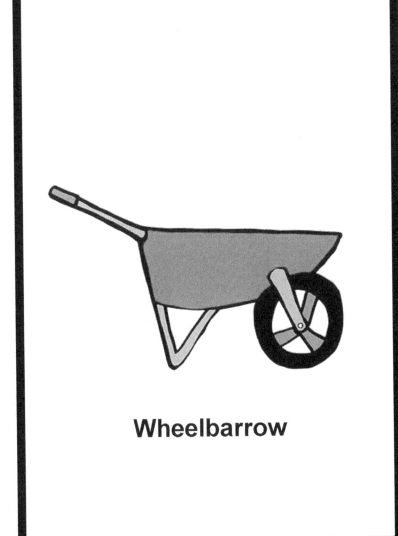

Wheelbarrow

ねこぐるま

Neko guru ma

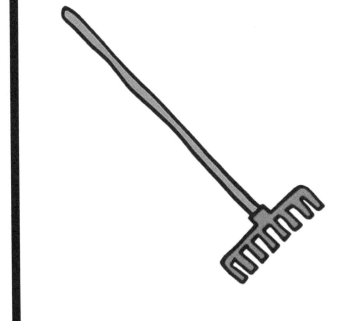

Rake

さらえ

Sarae

FLASHCARD BOOKS

NUMBERS
SHAPES & COLORS

ENGLISH
to
JAPANESE

FLASHCARD BOOK

BLACK & WHITE EDITION

One

いち

Ichi

Two

2

に

Ni

Three

さん

San

Four

4

し／よん

Shi/ Yon

Five

ご

Go

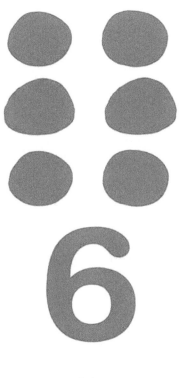

Six

6

ろく

Roku

Seven

しち／なな

Shichi/ Nana

Eight

はち

Hachi

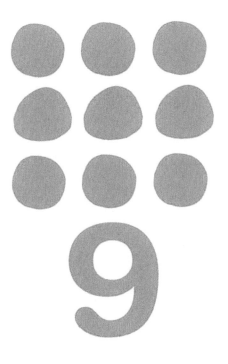

Nine

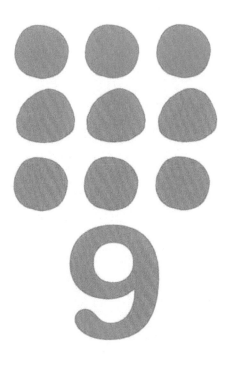

9

く／きゅう

Ku/ Kyuu

Ten

10

じゅう

Juu

Eleven

11

じゅういち

Juuichi

Twelve

12

じゅうに

Juuni

Thirteen

じゅうさん

Juusan

Fourteen

14

じゅうし／じゅうよん

Juusi/ Juuyon

Fifteen

じゅうご

Juugo

Sixteen

16

じゅうろく

Juuroku

Seventeen

じゅうしち／じゅうなな

Juushichi/ Juunana

Eighteen

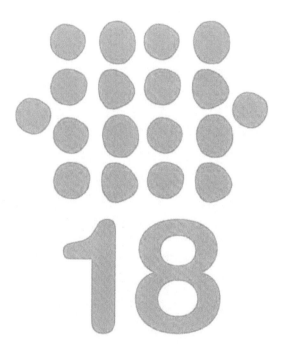

じゅうはち

Juuhachi

Nineteen

19

じゅうく／じゅうきゅう

Juuku/ Juukyuu

20

Twenty

20

にじゅう

Nijuu

Thirty

30

さんじゅう

Sanjuu

Forty

40

よんじゅう

Yonjuu

50

Fifty

50

ごじゅう

Gojuu

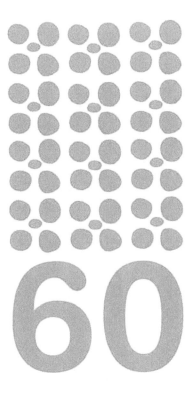

Sixty

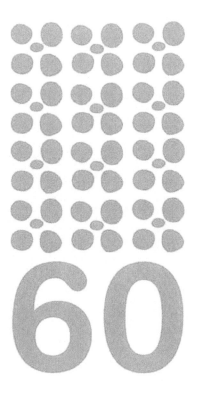

60

ろくじゅう

Rokujuu

Seventy

70

ななじゅう

Nanajuu

Eighty

80

はちじゅう

Hachijuu

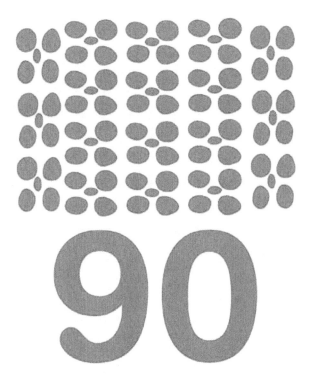

90

Ninety

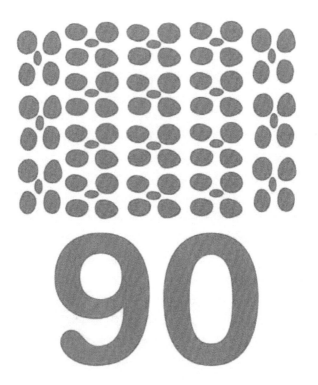

90

きゅうじゅう

Kyuujuu

100

One Hundred

100

ひゃく

Hyaku

1,000

One thousand

1,000

せん

Sen

1,000,000

One Million

1,000,000

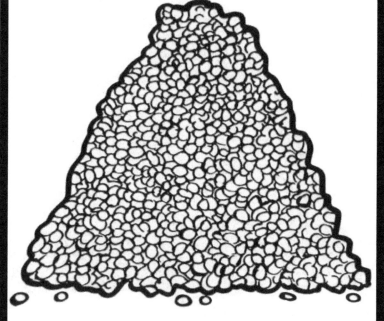

ひゃくまん

Hyakuman

Red

あか

Aka

Yellow

きいろ

Kiiro

Pink

ぴんく

Pinku

Blue

あお

Ao

Black

くろ

Kuro

White

しろ

Shiro

Brown

ちゃいろ

Chairo

Green

みどり

Midori

Orange

おれんじ

Orenji

Grey

はいいろ

Haiiro

Purple

むらさき

Murasaki

Square

しかく／せいほうけい

Shikaku/Seihoukei

Triangle

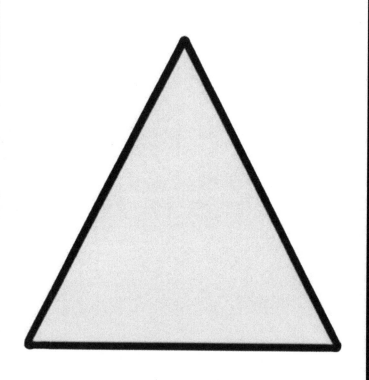

さんかく／さんかくけい

Sankaku/Sankakukei

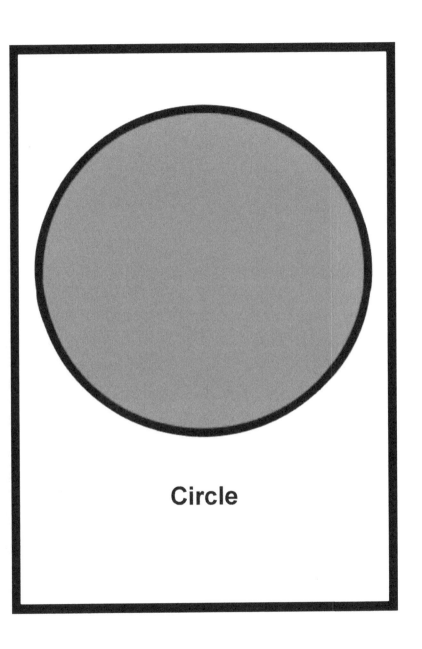

Circle

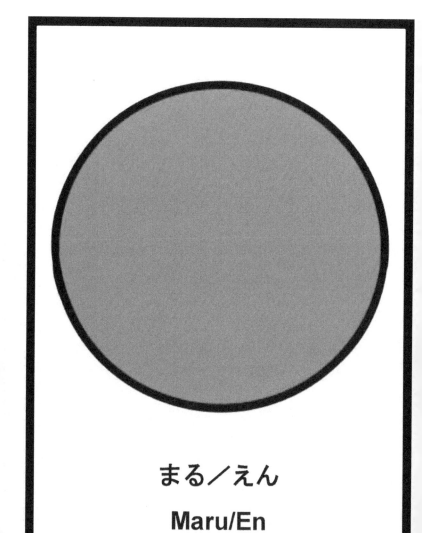

まる／えん

Maru/En

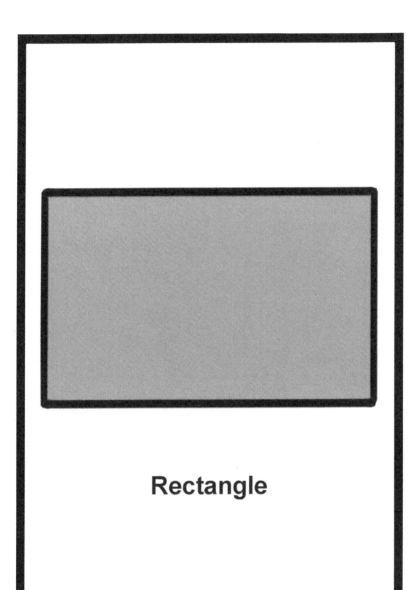

Rectangle

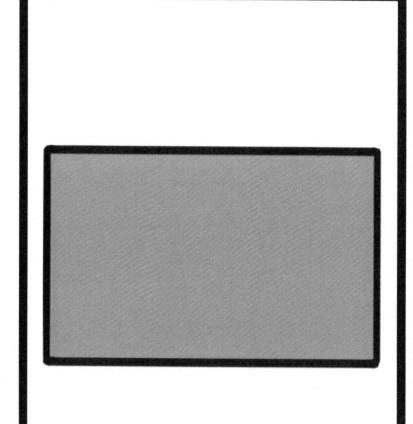

ちょうほうけい

Chouhoukei

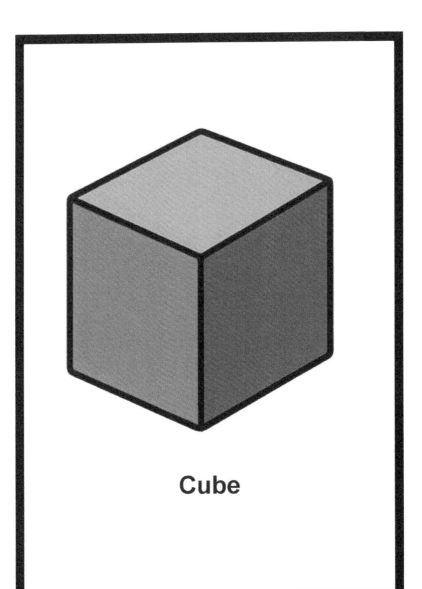

Cube

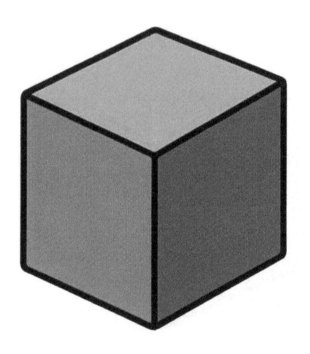

りっぽうたい

Rippoutai

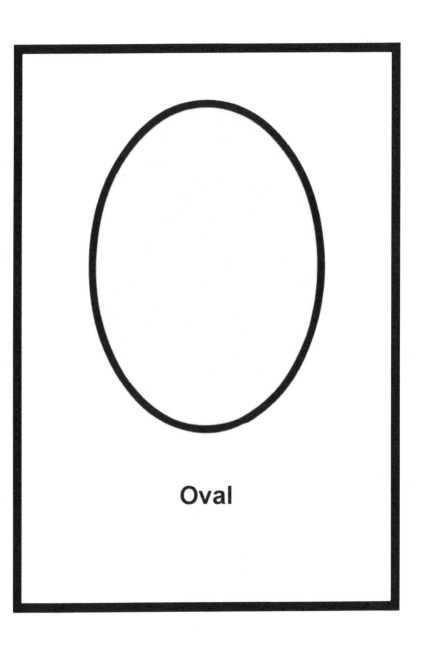

Oval

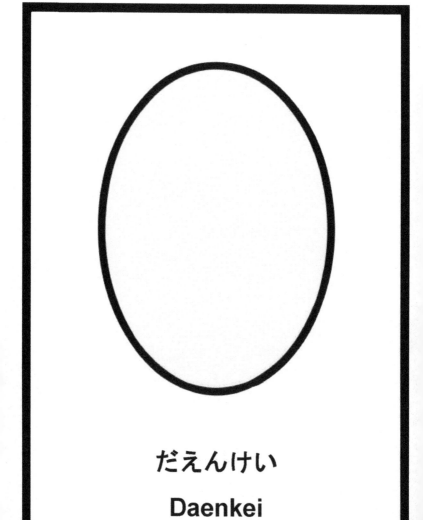

だえんけい

Daenkei

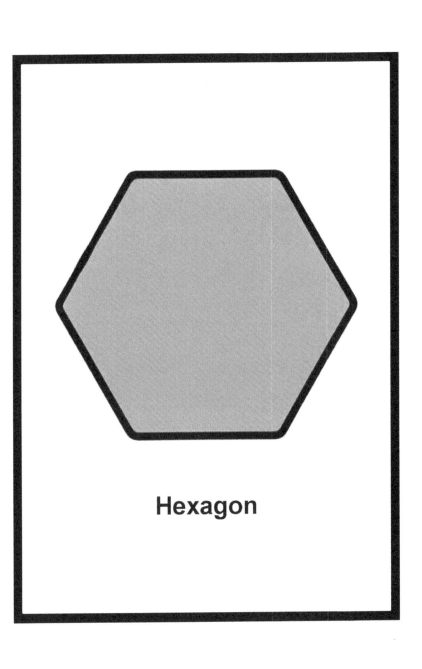

Hexagon

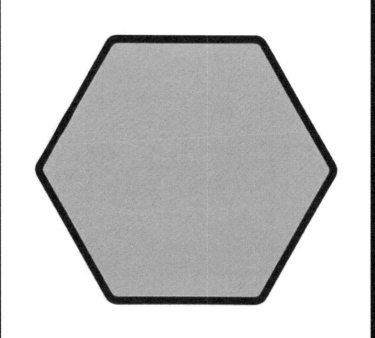

ろっかくけい

Rokkakukei

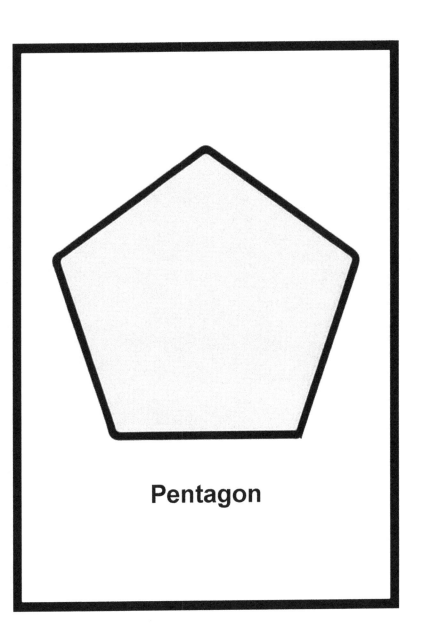

Pentagon

ごかくけい

Gokakukei

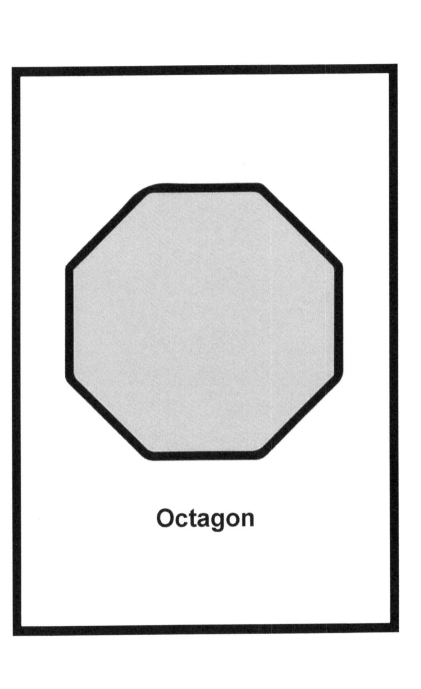

Octagon

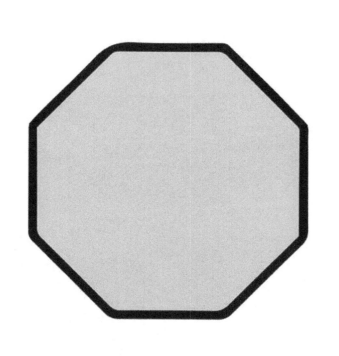

はっかくけい

Hakkakukei

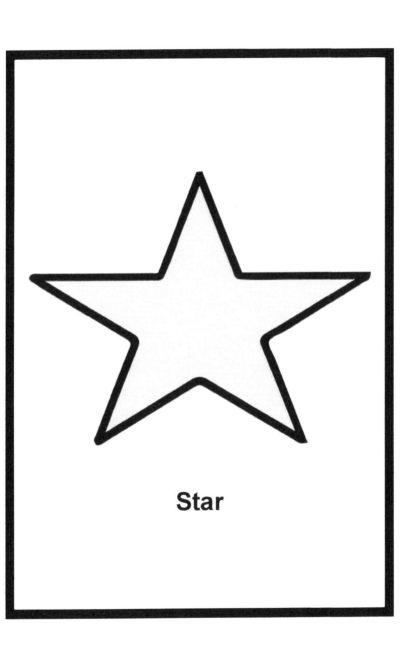

Star

ほし

Hoshi

Heart

はーと

Ha-to

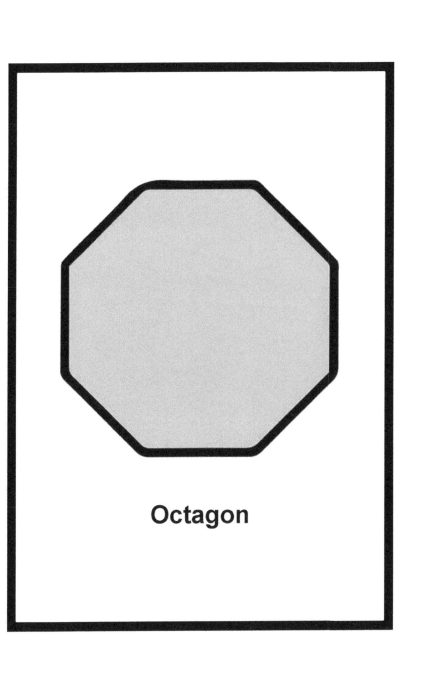

Octagon

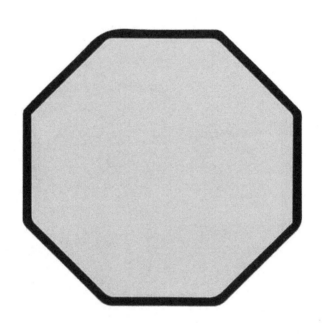

はっかくけい

Hakkakukei

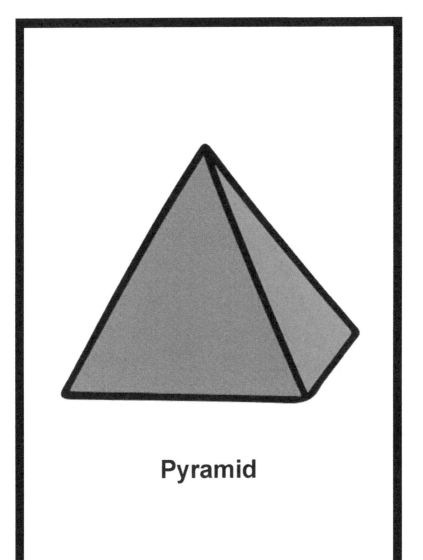

Pyramid

かくすい

Kakusui

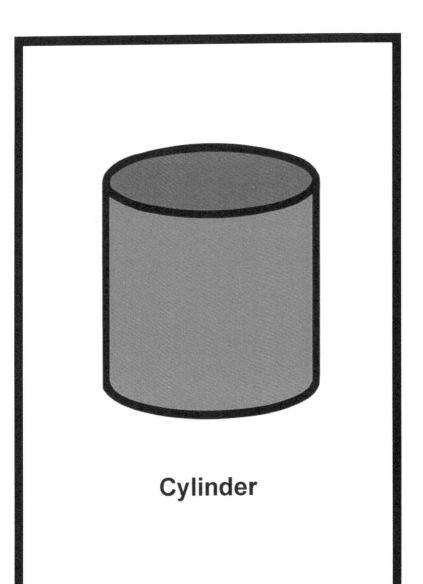

Cylinder

えんちゅう

Enchuu

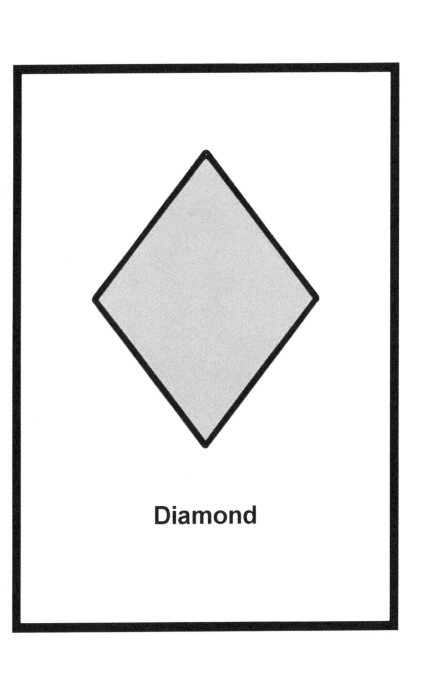

Diamond

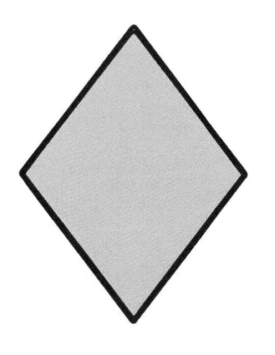

ひしがた
Hishigata

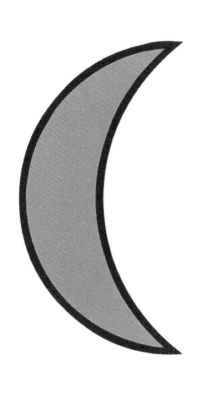

Crescent

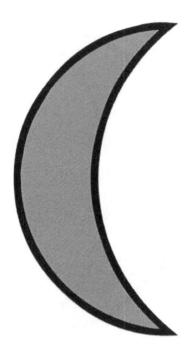

みかづき

Mikazuki

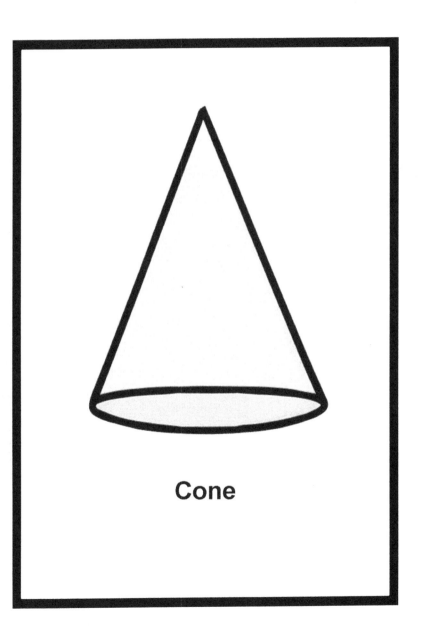

Cone

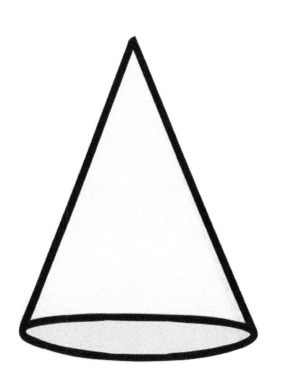

えんすい

Ensui

Made in the USA
Middletown, DE
28 September 2023